To: ______________________________

From: ______________________________

"I wish for you a life of wealth, health and happiness; a life in which you give to yourself the gift of patience, the virtue of reason, the value of knowledge, and the influence of faith in your own ability to dream about and to achieve worthy rewards."

—Jim Rohn

Published by SUCCESS
200 Swisher Road
Lake Dallas, Texas 75065
Toll-free: 866-SUCCESS (782-2377)
www.SUCCESS.com

Printed in the United States of America.
Book design by Sam Watson and Floro Torres.
ISBN 978-1-935944-07-2

SPECIAL SALES

SUCCESS books are available at special discounts for bulk purchase for sales promotions and premiums. Special editions, including personalized covers, excerpts of existing books, and corporate imprints, can be created in large quantities for special needs. For more information, contact Special Markets, SUCCESS, sales@success.com.

THE JIM ROHN GUIDE TO COMMUNICATION

JIM ROHN

For more than 40 years, Jim Rohn honed his craft like a skilled artist, helping people all over the world sculpt life strategies that expanded their imagination of what is possible. Jim set the standard for those who seek to teach and inspire others. He possessed the unique ability to bring extraordinary insights to ordinary principles and events. Those who had the privilege of hearing him speak can attest to the elegance and common sense in his material. It is no coincidence, then, that he is widely regarded as one of the most influential thinkers of our time and a national treasure. Jim authored numerous books and audio and video programs, and he helped motivate and shape an entire generation of personal development trainers and hundreds of executives from America's top corporations.

For additional information or to shop for Jim Rohn's best-selling books, CDs, DVDs and more, go to www.JimRohn.com.

➤ A NOTE ON THIS GUIDE ➤

The text of this pocket-size guide is based on transcripts of Jim Rohn's most popular lectures and writings on the subject of communication. His original words have been transcribed, edited, rearranged and slightly modified in some instances for greater clarity.

As you read, you may recognize a familiar pace to the text. It is our hope that Jim's easy conversational tone and speaking style come across in your reading of each and every page. Though some of Jim's references may be out of date, his life philosophies and success principles transcend the years and are as relevant today as they were when he first expressed them.

The intent of this guide is to provide a concise, easy-to-read treatment of the subject matter that can be read in a short sitting of 15 to 20 minutes. Highlight your favorite parts and keep it close for easy reference again and again. Share it with friends, family, associates, clients and anyone you feel would benefit from the timeless wisdom of a true legend.

See page 48 for information on other booklets in the Jim Rohn Guide series.

THE JIM ROHN GUIDE TO COMMUNICATION

Effective communication is a critical component of mastering success. By mastering the art of communication, you'll increase every level of performance in your life. I've often said that if you just communicate, you can get by. But if you communicate skillfully, you can work miracles—miracles in your family relationships, your business relationships and your friendships. Take advantage of every opportunity to practice your communication skills so that when important occasions arise, you will have the gift, the style, the sharpness, the clarity and the emotions to affect other people. What a unique opportunity to touch others with something small but powerful—our words.

Now, before we get to the fundamentals of effective communication, there's some groundwork to be laid. You see, preparation is the key to good communication. You've got to make deliberate, consistent effort to keep putting into your head, and putting into your heart and soul, valuable information from your life experiences. You can't speak that which you don't know. You can't relate what you don't have. You can't give out what hasn't come in. So the first key to good communication is a consistent way to gather information, knowledge, experience, and then remember it, store it, and have it available so that you can use it. And preparation is the key.

› PREPARE TO COMMUNICATE ‹

Now to prepare for good communication, I've got four words for you. Here they are:

1. Interest

Sharpen your curiosity and your interest in life and people. Those are the big subjects: life and people. What about life? The questions you might have about life and the mysteries of life. What about people and human behavior? People ask me, "Mr. Rohn, when you go to Russia are the people there the same as they are in America?" And the answer is "Yes."

Everywhere I go around the world, from South Africa to Northern Ireland, people are the same. What they want is the same. They would like to be employed. They'd like to have something to do. They'd like to have a way to earn their way. They'd like to make a good living. They'd like to supply incredible values for their family, and plan for the future—not only for the next generation but the next generation after. They'd like to make a contribution to the community and to their country. They'd like to be valuable in more than one respect. They'd like to be good parents. They'd like to leave a legacy. The list is the same whether you go to Siberia or to Australia. It doesn't make any difference. We all have those kinds of ambitions. In some countries, of course, the opportunity to do so is a lot better than in other countries that are struggling with just survival, let alone succeeding.

You should sharpen your interest and keep a journal of your impressions when you visit another city or when you visit another region. I go to Australia and if it's raining they say, "Bring your brelly." That means umbrella. They've got all these unique words. So when you go to Australia, when you go to other countries, you pick up on this because it's interesting. It's interesting conversation, and if you know a little about this, it's fascinating. The key is to just sharpen your interest in life and people, and region and country, and nation and ceremonies, and style and expressions, and all that.

You just pick up all of that flavor and the style and the language and the idiosyncrasies of wherever you go. You pick all that up as preparation so that your conversation will be more interesting to someone else. And you can flavor it with the color of your experiences of where you've been and what you've seen and what you've heard.

2. Fascination

Go from interested to fascinated. Interested people want to know, does it work? Fascinated people want to know, how does it work? What goes on below the surface? I can see that it works, but what makes it work?

Kids have this extraordinary ability to ask these questions. They can ask a hundred an hour. It's amazing. It's because they want to know. Their minds are just zinging all the time. Questions about what's happening and what's going on and how does it work and why is it this way and how come it works like this? That's so valuable in preparing to store in your mental bank and your bank of experiences more and more information, more and more experiences, colored and flavored by your own emotional content so that when you get ready to speak, you have something valuable to say.

Day by day, let life fascinate you. Let life interest you. Substitute fascination in place of frustration. I used to be frustrated, now I'm fascinated. It's a little trick you just have to play, but I've gotten pretty good at it. I'm on the freeway in Los Angeles. My airplane leaves in 35 minutes. The traffic's moving not one inch. I'm now fascinated. I'm telling you now, it doesn't work every time. Nothing works every time. But every time you can get it to work, let something fascinate you instead of frustrate you. Be curious how life works. That's how you gather more from your life experiences and prepare for good communication.

3. Sensitivity

The next word, and this is an important word in preparing for communication, is *sensitivity*. Try to put yourself in someone else's shoes. Try to feel what they feel. Try to hurt like they hurt. Have sympathy and compassion.

Sensitivity is trying to understand where someone might be at the moment. The reason that they're angry may not be obvious. Maybe the IRS just knocked on their door a couple days ago. That's why they're upset. You can't just go by what's obvious because there might be some reasons behind the reasons. So you've got to learn to be a little more sympathetic, a little more understanding. This is vitally important. Sometimes it's difficult, unless you are like that person, to sympathize or to have sensitivity. But here's what you must do: You must try. People know when you try.

I go to Mexico and try to speak a little Spanish. I listen to music on this great Spanish station in Los Angeles. If you just try to understand, try to speak a few words, it goes such a long way in identifying with people, in building a bridge of understanding and getting something started toward good communications.

4. Knowledge

So we've got interest, we've got fascination, and we've got sensitivity. Here's one more word: *knowledge*. You just have to know. Collect knowledge in your journal, from your ongoing education. Fill up your mental and spiritual and emotional bank so that it becomes like an unending reservoir to draw from. That begins to help you prepare. Do your research. Gather up stories. Keep the flow of knowledge going into your journal, as well as into your head and into your heart.

➤ THE FUNDAMENTALS OF EFFECTIVE COMMUNICATION ➤

Our very success is heavily dependent upon our ability to communicate. This is not just for professional speakers. From schoolchildren to grandparents, everyone should work on improving their communication skills so they can improve their lives. Improving your ability to communicate will be one of the most important things you ever do.

One of the easiest ways to improve your communication is to start by solidifying your base, so to speak, by working on and improving the fundamentals. Here are a few areas that everyone should know and master.

› COMMUNICATION IS POWERFUL ‹

There is a proverb in the Bible that says, "The tongue has the power of life and death." This is true. What a person says can build people up or tear them down. The ability to communicate is a powerful responsibility. Whole nations have been inspired to action because of a single individual's passionate words. On the other hand, countless millions of children have been deeply hurt because of the derogatory words spoken to them by their parents. You have within you the incredible power of communication. You can create tremendous things in your life if you take communication seriously and use its power to help others and yourself. Combining this knowledge with a heart set on doing good is the first step in unleashing this incredible force.

➤ COMMUNICATION MUST BE PURPOSEFUL ➤

In order to be effective, your communication should be on purpose. Yes, occasionally you may say something off the top of your head and that can hold weight with others, but this is the exception and not the rule. In order to become an effective communicator, you should be very purposeful about your communication. Know what you want to communicate, when you want to communicate and how you want to communicate. Decide what kind of communication will enhance your life and the lives of those around you, and plan your steps for communicating in that way. And then work your plan—know what it is you want to accomplish and how you must communicate in order to do so.

➤ WHAT YOU SAY MUST MATCH WHAT YOU DO ➤

Remember, people watch what you do, not just what you say. What you do always outweighs what you say. If you say one thing and do another, people will follow what you do. If you say something and back it up with your actions, you will provide the "proof" for people who are listening to you, and they will much more willingly follow your lead.

➤ IMPROVE YOUR SPEAKING AND WRITING ➤

When it comes to communication, these are the "Big Two" that everyone can improve upon: speaking and writing. For every one step that you take to increase your ability to speak and write, you'll improve your career position two steps. Don't think that you have to become the best speaker or writer in the world; just set your sights on the next level above where you are now. Once you get there, continue to work to the next level.

Here are a few tips for becoming a better speaker:

- Join Toastmasters
- Take a college course on public speaking
- Give a speech in front of a mirror
- Just speak—wherever you can

Here are a few tips for becoming a better writer:

- Keep a journal
- Join a writing club
- Have people who are more skilled than you help edit (and critique) your letters and emails
- Take a college course on writing
- Write that book you've been thinking about

Becoming a better speaker and writer will be based

on three things: doing it, getting feedback and acting on that feedback.

› LEARN TO LISTEN ‹

Communication is not one direction—it goes both ways. To become an effective communicator, you must be a good listener. All of the following examples show the power of listening:

- The parent who listens for the feelings of his or her child
- The salesperson who listens for what kind of product the client wants
- The boss who listens to the concerns of his or her employees

Can you see how listening in those situations enables you to become a better communicator? Once you know what your "audience" wants, you will be able to better communicate to them.

➤ SHOW THAT YOU CARE ◄

Talk with people, not to them. People don't want you to talk at them. They want to communicate. Think about it. The root word is *commune*, which means to live and share together. This is what we do when we communicate together—we share words and ideas. This means we must care about the people we are communicating with. We should be interested in their needs and desires. And when we know those, we can communicate more effectively with them.

➤ FOCUS ON CLARITY ◄

The most effective communication is clear communication. Many beginning speakers believe that they should be as verbose as possible—but that's not what makes them effective. The important principle is clarity. Do they (the people in your audience) understand your message? That is the question. If they don't, then you haven't communicated. Be as clear and as concise as you can. Never go any longer than it takes to make the communication as clear as it needs to be. And, above all, make sure your audience understands your message when you are finished.

➤ COMMUNICATE OVER AND OVER AGAIN ➤

In order to be effective, communication must be done over and over again. The parent or boss who yells, "How many times must I tell you?" is really just proving again that people need to hear a message many times before they internalize it. That is just the difficult nature of communication. Very rarely will you be able to communicate something just once and have someone or some group walk away with full understanding. It just doesn't happen that way. You need to do it often and in varied ways. This is what will make your communication most effective.

➤ IMPROVE YOUR VOCABULARY, PRONUNCIATION AND SPELLING ➤

When people hear you or read what you have written, they look for class and style. This can often be noticed through your vocabulary, your pronunciation and your spelling. If you want to be more effective, focus on improving in these areas. Our vocabulary directly affects the way we both view and interpret the world around us. If we have a small vocabulary, it limits our ability to define or communicate what we see, feel and hear. The larger the vocabulary, the better our ability to relate. What size is your view—a peephole or a huge, clear window showing the great expanse of this amazing, wonderful world we live in?

➤ THE BASICS OF BUSINESS COMMUNICATION ➤

The goals of business relationships differ from the goals of personal relationships, although they do entail utilizing some of the same interpersonal skills.

The goals of business relationships are the following:

1. Build positive working relationships that allow us to work together for profitable, win/win business dealings
2. Enhance the value of work production
3. Create win-win, mutually satisfying business opportunities
4. Produce a profit while providing the marketplace with value through our goods and services

So, if the above are the goals of business relationships, then the goal of our business communications should support the overarching goal of the business relationship.

Here are four qualifying questions that will help form guidelines necessary to accomplish this:

1. Does our business communication support positive working relationships?

2. Does our business communication support the value of the other party?
3. Does our business communication support win-win relationships?
4. Does our business communication support profit-making ventures and value to the marketplace?

In our communication with people (our employees, vendors, clients), our constant goal should be to uphold those basic values, in all aspects. It's easy to do this with a client who has just made a large purchase. It's far more difficult, but equally important, when we're working with someone challenging. The idea is to be so in tune with our goals that it affects how we communicate with those with whom we do business.

FIVE FORMS OF BUSINESS COMMUNICATION

Now I want to talk a bit about different kinds of communication and some tips to improving your skills.

There are five basic forms of communication in business today.

1. In Person: One-on-One

One-on-one meetings are very effective if done properly. The obvious downside is the limitation of time, especially if you have numerous people you need to meet with.

Here are some ideas to make your one-on-one meetings more effective:

- **Brief the person you are meeting with beforehand on the topic.** This defines the basic expectations of the purpose of the meeting and maximizes the time you have. More will be accomplished, and it prevents the possibility of having to schedule a follow-up meeting.
- **Be on time and end on time.** This is paramount and communicates that you value the other person's time.

- **Meet in an appropriate setting.** Sometimes a coffee shop may be appropriate. Other times you will need to be in a meeting room. Take into account who the other person is, what you are hoping to accomplish and how much time you have. Is the meeting place conducive to communication? Be sure your chosen location enhances, not detracts, so that the possibility of missed communication is greatly reduced or eliminated.
- **Practice good communication skills.** Listening skills, speaking clearly, etc., are vital skills you need to put into practice here.
- **Sum up.** At the end of the meeting, take a moment to sum up what you think you have heard and what you have attempted to communicate.
- **Follow up.** This can be done with an email, a note card or phone call. Again, sum up what you spoke about and be sure to thank them for their time and the opportunity to meet with them.

2. In Person: Group Meetings

Brief the group beforehand on the topic. Just as with one-on-one settings, this creates expectations, enables everyone to be prepared and will maximize everyone's time.

- **Again, start on time and end on time.** A dual purpose is accomplished here—this communicates that you value their time and it says that no one person is more important than the group.
- **Appoint a note taker.** One person should be in charge of putting the information on a whiteboard or AV screen while the meeting is in progress. This is an improvement over the traditional way of someone taking notes on paper because the meeting participants can see how the topics are being recorded and can immediately make corrections if there is misinterpretation.
- **Give everyone an opportunity to participate.** Be diligent in keeping one or two people from dominating the meeting. Make sure you ask for the

input of everyone. If they are valued enough to be invited to the meeting, their views are important.

- **Stay on task.** The biggest time-waster of meetings is the proverbial "rabbit trail." As the leader, or even if you're just attending the meeting, you should be willing, when the topic veers off course, to encourage the group to get back to the purpose of the meeting.

3. The Phone

The phone has wonderful applications for communication. There are some roadblocks with the proliferation of voice mail, but the phone still remains a great tool for communication.

Here are some tips for making the phone work for your business communication.

- **Use it to keep in touch.** The great thing about a phone is you can pick it up, dial and be connected with someone in just moments. Use the phone to stay in regular communication with your business contacts. A quick call to see how they are doing or to ask how you might be of help to them will not only bring you business but also raise your profile in their mind as a person who provides great customer service and follow-up.

- **Schedule times for phone meetings.** Sometimes, just picking up the phone is ineffective because the person you're trying to reach will not be able to talk at that time. If they aren't available right then, take just a second and set up a time to speak with them. Ask them to schedule a time to speak by phone and then record it in your calendar or planner. The longer the time you need, the more advance notice you'll need to give them.
- **Know what you're calling for.** In personal relationships, people are much more willing to sit around and "shoot the breeze," but not so much in business relationships. "Time is money," as the old saying goes. Instead, with business relationships, we should tell the person we'll be speaking

with what the topic will be and what we hope to accomplish. This should be done beforehand. Then stick to the topic and don't digress.

- **Don't take too much time.** The phone can also become a real time waster for both you and the people you speak with if you're not careful. If you know what you want to accomplish and discipline yourself to stick to the agenda, you'll be able to limit your time and be very efficient with the use of the phone.

4. Written Communications

The written word is still very effective for communication. It can be more powerful than the spoken word in some instances because it can be edited before being released. In addition, it can be referred to again.

Some tips for written communications:

- **Keep it simple.** Obviously there are some communications that need to be long and complex—elaborate contracts, for example—but for the most part, our business communications should be very pragmatic. That is, they should simply get the job done; there's no need for trying to be too eloquent.
- **Use various forms to keep interest alive.** A memo, a note card, a letter and email all are different methods that'll entice the reader to read. Varying methods can help our message be communicated better.

5. The Speech

At times, you'll be called upon to speak to an audience. This can be a powerful form of communication that'll help build your business and your relationships.

› COMMUNICATION TOOLS ‹

Some people use the phrase "the art of communication," and I like that phrase. Communicating is an art. When we're attempting to get our message out to others, it's as though we start with a giant blank canvas and we then begin to paint a picture—any picture we desire.

Now, most people assume that when painting a picture they have only a few basic brushes at their disposal. But the advanced artist knows there are many tools available to create their masterpiece, and they use each to their advantage.

The same is true with communication. There are many tools available to you as you communicate; you just have to be aware of them and then use them purposefully. The better you become at using these tools, the better you'll be at communicating.

The two primary categories these tools fall into are verbal and nonverbal. Let's look at the different ways you can use each of these categories to improve your ability to communicate.

➤ VERBAL COMMUNICATION ➤

Your words. It's been said that people judge you by the words you use, and this is true. Choose your words wisely. Words have power. They have the power to move nations and they have the power to destroy as well. When you speak, use words carefully.

Here are a few things to consider in regard to your words.

- Avoid using words that will cause the other person to think poorly of you. Slang is one example. Another is, of course, slurs of any type. Use words that communicate positive values. Use optimistic words, words of strength. Make sure they are understandable.

- Use words that are colorful and rich with meaning, as long as they can be understood by the listener.

Your vocabulary. An expanded vocabulary will set you apart. It enhances the communication process and draws others in.

Your vocabulary can reveal to others how educated you are, and others may make judgments about you that can affect your opportunities with them. The best communicators will use an expanded vocabulary with more educated groups and a more basic vocabulary with less-educated groups.

› HOW YOU SAY IT MATTERS ‹

Just as important as what you say is how you say it. What tone are you using? When you speak, are you monotone? Or do you move the tone of your voice, changing it up? This will naturally help people follow what you're saying. Changing the tone of your voice is a very effective way to draw people into your message. Imagine if a painter only used one color. We want lots of color and lots of tone.

Along with the words you use and your tone, consider your pace. Sometimes when you speak you may need to go slowly, and sometimes you may need to go very fast. The speed with which you speak will tell others certain things. A fast pace will communicate that you're excited about something. A slow pace usually communicates thoughtfulness or that you really want them to hear your point.

Choosing your pace is also like using your volume in an effective way. Master communicators will draw their audience in by fluctuating their voice from very loud to a near whisper. The audience doesn't even know that the speaker is taking them on a roller-coaster ride of communication. There are lessons to be learned here. Even in a one-on-one conversation, we can shift and change volume, keeping our communication more effective.

› EMOTION ‹

The emotions you communicate while speaking are vital. The key here is to show emotion without "getting emotional." Emotions can be a very effective communicator. For example, showing anger can communicate that you are very serious about something (as long as you don't get angry often). Allowing yourself to cry can show a side of you to others that communicates that you are a person of passion who, while being a hard-charging person who desires success, also has a tender side. Allowing yourself to laugh will communicate that you have a fun side and do not take yourself too seriously. Emotion, if controlled, is a powerful communicator.

› ENUNCIATION ‹

Do you speak clearly so people can understand you? Enunciation is an often-overlooked key to effective communication. It's imperative to clearly enunciate our words so that people understand us. Clear enunciation gives us a little "punch" to our communication. Work on enunciating your words clearly. The key is to get it just right—enunciating so that your words don't run together but not over-enunciating so that you sound unnatural.

In all of these principles, the idea is variety. Any time we communicate in a single way, we become predictable and people stop listening. Think of yourself. Do you like to listen to people who speak at one speed, in one tone, with a boring vocabulary and without emotion? Of course not! Then we should make every effort to be colorful and effective communicators. And we can be—if we work at it and practice, practice, practice!

NONVERBAL COMMUNICATION

What you say affects how you communicate, certainly, but just as important is what you don't say. Yes, your nonverbal communication has a major impact on how well you communicate.

Have you ever given much thought to how you communicate nonverbally? Here are some thoughts on ways to use nonverbal communication to support what you're saying verbally.

- **Use your hands.** Keeping your hands by your side will make you seem stiff and uncomfortable. Instead, use your hands to communicate. Now, don't get too demonstrative to the point where people are wondering where your hands are going next. One way to see what you do nonverbally is to tape yourself speaking. Watch what you do with your hands.
- **Use your eyes.** The eyes can be a very powerful tool in communication. You know

the old saying, "The eyes are the window into the soul." It's true. Think of what a mother communicates to her newborn when she gazes into their eyes, or what a husband and a wife say without words when they look into each other's eyes. The eyes speak volumes.

Have you spoken with someone who is constantly looking around? What does that communicate? A lack of interest in what you have to say.

When you speak to someone, look at them. Give them your attention with your eyes. Listen to them with your eyes. Communicate with them that they are important.

- **Your arms.** Some people don't even realize when they're "closed off" to someone else by crossing their arms when the other person is speaking. Those who study this tell us that crossing the arms is a surefire way to close yourself off from the other person. It communicates closure, fear and opposition.

- **Speaking position.** When you're communicating, especially in a presentation situation, your speaking position, whether you are standing, sitting, kneeling, etc., can communicate a lot.

  For example, my good friend Zig Ziglar, a master of the stage, will frequently move to the front of the stage and kneel. What is he nonverbally communicating? He is saying, "Listen closely to this. This is really important." He is bringing the audience in for an "intimate moment." Even in a room with 1,000 people, this way of communicating can make every individual feel like Zig is speaking closely to just them.

  Sitting communicates casualness. I know many speakers will give a considerable part of their presentation this way. John C. Maxwell, another friend of mine, and a world-class leadership expert, gives quite a bit of his speeches while sitting. His style is informative and casual—and it is effective.

➤ OTHER NONVERBAL CONSIDERATIONS ◂

There are other little things to be aware of in nonverbal communications. Nodding your head says, "I'm listening." Tapping your foot or jiggling your leg says, "I'm bored, nervous or impatient." Everything we do with our bodies communicates, whether we're speaking or listening.

As a person who desires to take their communication to the next level, you should be aware of what you communicate nonverbally as well as verbally. As you begin to master both, you'll begin to communicate with a higher and higher level of excellence.

➤ SEVEN ESSENTIALS FOR POWERFUL AND EFFECTIVE PRESENTATIONS ◂

Follow these seven rules, and you will begin to see greater effectiveness in your presentations.

1. Know your goal

Are you there to inspire? Encourage? Challenge? Comfort? Motivate? Deliver bad news? Good news? Is it just informational? Are you trying to motivate them to action? If you know where you're going and where you want to take the audience, you can then work back from there and create your presentation. Like Stephen Covey's old axiom, "Begin with the end in mind," be sure to know your goal.

2. Keep it simple

Be yourself—you don't have to be someone else. One mistake many people make is in trying to emulate the style of another person. This rarely, if ever, works. Why? Because you're not that person! Be yourself. That is who others are expecting.

Don't attempt elaborate presentations. Maybe when you've mastered your skills, you can get elaborate. But even the most polished professional speakers rarely get elaborate. The Zig Ziglars, Brian Tracys and Nido Qubeins of the world—the crème de la crème—are straight-ahead, no-fancy-stuff speakers. Take note of that. You can be simple and very good at the same time. So be sure to keep it simple.

3. Be passionate and optimistic about your topic

People want to see that you are passionate about your topic. Aristotle said that there are three areas integral to persuasion: logic, ethics and passion. You need to be a person of good character, have logical reasoning and say it with passion.

Also, be optimistic. Napoleon said, "Leaders are dealers in hope." As presenters, we pull people in and bring them along by giving them hope. Be sure to let your passion and optimism come through.

4. Balance the format of your information

Use facts, figures and stories. Include lecture as well as audience participation. In this day and age, with waning attention spans, we do well to change up the format on regular intervals. People are used to modern media, which makes single-person speaking a tough act. Be sure to use different formats in your presentation.

5. Tell stories

When you think of Jesus, the greatest teacher of all time, you think of a man who told stories to help root the principles into the minds and hearts of those who heard him. Stories are things that people can connect with. They can remember them. They see them in pictures. What would you be most apt to remember two weeks after hearing a speaker: the exact percentages of his or her statistics, or a well-told story? Be sure to build stories into your presentation so people remember the points you want them to.

6. Know your material

This is the foundation of an effective presentation. It tells people you're serious about the topic, that you care about it and that you're qualified to speak to them about it. Do whatever you can to know your material inside and out before you get on the stage to present. You'll feel more comfortable and will come across as very credible. Audiences are looking for credibility and can see through someone who is winging their way through a presentation. Be sure to know your material.

7. Start on time and end on time

One of the skills of an effective presenter is that they can craft their presentation to fit the allotted time and then discipline themselves to stay within that time frame. Starting on time and ending on time will show people that you respect their time.

Too often, a speaker will do a fine job in their allotted time, and if they were to end there, they would be remembered well. Unfortunately, they go overtime, and all the audience can think is, "I can't believe they went so long!" These speakers shoot themselves in the foot by not finishing on time. Be sure to always stay within your time limits and leave your audience wanting more.

I believe that everyone can become a better speaker and presenter if they practice their skill. And it doesn't require a tremendous amount of advanced training, either. Just mastering the basics will take you to the next level and allow you to become a much more effective communicator.

THE JIM ROHN GUIDE SERIES

The timeless wisdom of Jim Rohn in concise, easy-to-read guides. Perfect for sharing with friends, family, business associates, clients and prospects.

TIME MANAGEMENT
PERSONAL DEVELOPMENT
LEADERSHIP
GOAL SETTING
COMMUNICATION

Quantity discounts available
JimRohn.com or
store.SUCCESS.com